7/08

Biographies

Pancho Villa

Rebel of the Mexican Revolution

by Mary Englar

Consultants:
Colin M. MacLachlan
John Christy Barr Distinguished Professor of History
Tulane University
New Orleans, Louisiana

Erwin P. Grieshaber
Professor of History
Minnesota State University, Mankato
Mankato, Minnesota

Capstone press

Mankato, Minnesota

Fact Finders is published by Capstone Press,
151 Good Counsel Drive, P.O. Box 669, Mankato, Minnesota 56002.
www.capstonepress.com

Library of Congress Cataloging-in-Publication Data
Englar, Mary.
  Pancho Villa, rebel of the Mexican Revolution / by Mary Englar.
  p. cm. — (Fact finders. Biographies. Great Hispanics)
  Includes bibliographical references and index.
  ISBN-13: 978-0-7368-5441-2 (hardcover)
  ISBN-10: 0-7368-5441-X (hardcover)
  1. Villa, Pancho, 1878–1923—Juvenile literature. 2. Mexico—History—1910–1946—
Juvenile literature. 3. Revolutionaries—Mexico—Biography—Juvenile literature. I. Title.
II. Series.
F1234.V63E64 2006
972.08'1'092—dc22   2005022583

Summary: An introduction to the life of Pancho Villa, the Mexican outlaw who played an
    important role in the Mexican Revolution of 1910.

Editorial Credits
Megan Schoeneberger, editor; Juliette Peters, set designer; Linda Clavel and Scott Thoms,
    book designers; Wanda Winch, photo researcher/photo editor

Photo Credits
Corbis, 4–5, 19, 25; Bettmann, 1, 6, 22–23, 26
El Paso County Historical Society, 20–21
Getty Images Inc./Hulton Archive, 18, 27; Topical Press Agency, cover
Hemeroteca Nacional de Mexico, 11, 13
Library of Congress, 8–9
University of Texas at El Paso Library, Special Collections Department, 15, 17

1 2 3 4 5 6 11 10 09 08 07 06

Table of Contents

Chapter 1 Land and Liberty! 4

Chapter 2 Childhood 8

Chapter 3 Life as an Outlaw 12

Chapter 4 Mexican Revolution 16

Chapter 5 Marriage and War 20

Chapter 6 A Mexican Hero 24

Fast Facts 27

Time Line 28

Glossary 30

Internet Sites 31

Read More 31

Index 32

Land and Liberty!

The government supply train chugged north toward Ciudad Juárez, Mexico. At each stop, General Pancho Villa forced the engineer to **telegraph** his message. "All clear," the message said.

The message was a trick. More than 2,000 **rebel** soldiers hid in the train's coal cars. Villa and another rebel leader, Pascual Orozco, planned to attack the city.

At 2:00 in the morning on May 11, 1911, the train entered the city. The rebels jumped off and surprised the 4,000 government soldiers guarding the city. Three hours later, Villa and Orozco controlled Ciudad Juárez. They were one step closer to overthrowing the Mexican government.

A group of rebels stand with their weapons during the attack on Ciudad Juárez.

▲ Porfirio Díaz ruled Mexico from 1877 until 1880 and again from 1884 until 1911.

A Fight for Change

In the early 1900s, most Mexicans were very poor. Rich men owned most of the good land. Farmers couldn't afford to keep their land. They were forced to work for the rich landowners. Farmers could barely afford to feed their families.

Workers in cities weren't any better off. They worked 12 hours a day, six days a week, and made little money.

By the 1910s, Mexicans wanted change. The current president, Porfirio Díaz, had done little to help the farmers and workers.

Pancho Villa helped lead a **revolution** of the Mexican people. Mexicans fought for the land they had lost. They also fought for the freedom to vote for a new president.

By the end of the fighting in 1920, Villa had become a legend. His enemies called him a cruel **outlaw**. His friends called him a hero. Pancho Villa called himself a freedom fighter.

QUOTE

"Men will not forget that Pancho Villa was loyal to the cause of the people."
—Pancho Villa

Chapter 2

Childhood

Pancho Villa was born June 5, 1878, in northern Mexico. His parents named him Doroteo Arango. As an adult, he was known as Pancho Villa. But as a boy, everybody called him Doroteo.

Doroteo's parents worked on a large farm in the Mexican state of Durango. The Arango family did not own the land they farmed. The whole family, even Doroteo and his four younger brothers and sisters, worked for the landowner. From sunrise to sunset, they worked in the fields. The children did not go to school. The men and boys also helped raise cattle. Doroteo's mother planted a garden of corn and beans to feed her family.

Poorly paid farmworkers performed the daily tasks of caring for animals and growing crops on Mexican farms in the late 1800s.

Doroteo's family was very poor. When they needed food or clothing, they had to buy it on **credit**. They always owed more money to the store than they earned.

Man of the House

When Doroteo was 7, his father died. Doroteo took care of his mother and siblings. Doroteo liked to work, and he worked very hard. He loved horses and became a good rider. When he got older, he worked extra jobs to help his family. He learned how to rope cattle and round them up.

Doroteo Arango, who later became known as Pancho Villa, was about 16 years old in this photograph.

Chapter 3

Life as an Outlaw

Historians know few facts about Doroteo's early life. Doroteo liked to make up stories about his life. Many historians don't believe the stories Doroteo told.

According to Doroteo, one day he heard his sister and mother screaming. The farm owner had tried to hurt his younger sister. Doroteo was very angry. He borrowed a gun and shot the owner. The owner didn't die, but Doroteo ran away. He knew the owner might beat him, put him in jail, or even kill him.

Doroteo loved horses and was a skilled rider.

Doroteo got on a horse and rode into the nearby mountains. The next day, he asked friends if the owner was looking for him. His friends said the owner asked the police to find Doroteo.

Running from the Law

Doroteo was only 16 years old. He had no money or food. He joined some outlaws to earn money. The outlaws robbed trains and stole cattle and horses. The police hunted Doroteo. He could not go home, but he sent money to his family.

In 1900, the police caught Doroteo and forced him into the army. He hated being in the army. In 1902, he escaped and returned to Durango. Doroteo decided to change his name so that he could find a job. He took the name Francisco Villa. His friends called him Pancho.

Soldiers in the Mexican Army march in formation in the early 1900s.

Chapter 4

Mexican Revolution

Villa tried many jobs. He worked in a mine and built houses. He bought a small house in Chihuahua, Mexico, and tried to settle down. When he could not find work, Villa stole cattle or horses for money.

In the early 1900s, many Mexicans were unhappy with their president, Porfirio Díaz. Francisco Madero, a respected landowner, wanted to run against Díaz in 1910. He asked Díaz to allow fair elections. Díaz put Madero in jail, and Díaz won the election unfairly.

Francisco Madero was a popular landowner who used his wealth to run for president in 1910.

Villa Joins the Revolution

When Madero got out of jail, he fled to the United States. Madero called for Mexicans to fight against Díaz. Villa supported Madero. He gathered his outlaw friends and joined the fighting.

⬆ Villa led a large army of poor workers and farmers in the fight against Díaz.

For seven months, Villa led his fighters in many battles. He took good care of his men. They respected his brave leadership.

In May 1911, Villa joined Pascual Orozco in an attack on the city of Ciudad Juárez. Villa's men fought house by house. On May 11, the government soldiers gave up. Ten days later, President Díaz quietly left the capital and escaped from Mexico.

Madero held a new election. In October 1911, he became the president of Mexico.

Rebels fought to gain control of Ciudad Juárez from the government soldiers.

Chapter 5

Marriage and War

In May 1911, Villa married Luz Corral, a young woman from a nearby town. They moved into his house in Chihuahua, Mexico. Villa worked on making the house bigger.

Villa brought his brothers to Chihuahua too. Together, they set up four butcher shops. Villa was a good businessperson and earned respect for his success.

Civil War

In 1913, an army general, Victoriano Huerta, rose up against President Madero. Madero was killed. Villa gathered his soldiers to fight against Huerta. Generals from all over Mexico fought against each other in a civil war.

Villa married Luz Corral on May 29, 1911.

By 1914, Villa led an army of 40,000 soldiers. It was the largest army in northern Mexico.

Even with so many soldiers, Villa's army lost a large battle in April 1915. After that loss, Villa backed off. He moved his army north toward the U.S. border.

Attack on Columbus, New Mexico

In 1916, as his army began running out of supplies, Villa attacked the U.S. town of Columbus, New Mexico. They burned buildings and shot people. Eighteen Americans died.

The United States sent 3,000 soldiers into Mexico to search for Villa. They never caught him.

General Villa Retires

In 1920, General Álvaro Obregón became president. He gave Villa a large ranch and a general's **pension** to stop fighting.

Villa's new ranch in Durango covered more than 160,000 acres (64,750 hectares). At first, only three rooms in the house had roofs. Villa rebuilt the house, the stables, and the storage buildings. He also built a school for the children of his workers.

◀ Villa rides alongside his army before a 1914 battle.

Chapter 6

A Mexican Hero

Villa knew he had many enemies. He feared that somebody might try to kill him. He gave every ranch worker a gun. Fifty men protected Villa wherever he went. Villa never left the ranch without his guards.

In July 1923, Villa made a business trip to Parral, Mexico. He took only the four guards who could fit in his car. After he finished his business, he started to drive home.

A man on the side of the road waved and called out to him. Then, several armed men fired more than 40 bullets into Villa's car. Villa was killed instantly.

Villa stopped fighting and moved to a large ranch.

As leader of the rebels, Villa helped change the Mexican government.

QUOTE

"Adios, General Villa.
Great hero among the heroes,
this singer will never forget you.
Rest among the dead,
in the world of other beings,
and if there is glory,
may you rest in eternal peace."
—Mexican folk song

Thousands of people came to Villa's funeral the next day. Villa received military honors for his service to Mexico.

Legacy

Villa was a bandit and a thief. In war, he was cruel. He killed many people while fighting for his cause.

But his fighting led to Mexico's revolution, and the revolution helped change the country. Mexicans gained a greater voice in their government. Workers got better pay and working conditions. Today, some Mexicans remember Villa as a hero of the revolution.

Fast Facts

Full name: Born Doroteo Arango. Changed his name to Francisco "Pancho" Villa.

Birth: June 5, 1878

Death: July 20, 1923

Parents: Augustin Arango and Maria Micaela Arambula

Siblings: 2 sisters, 2 brothers

Home: Born in the state of Durango, Mexico

Wife: Luz Corral

Children: 1 daughter

Achievements:
Rose to the rank of general in the revolutionary army
Led 40,000 men during Mexico's civil war

Time Line

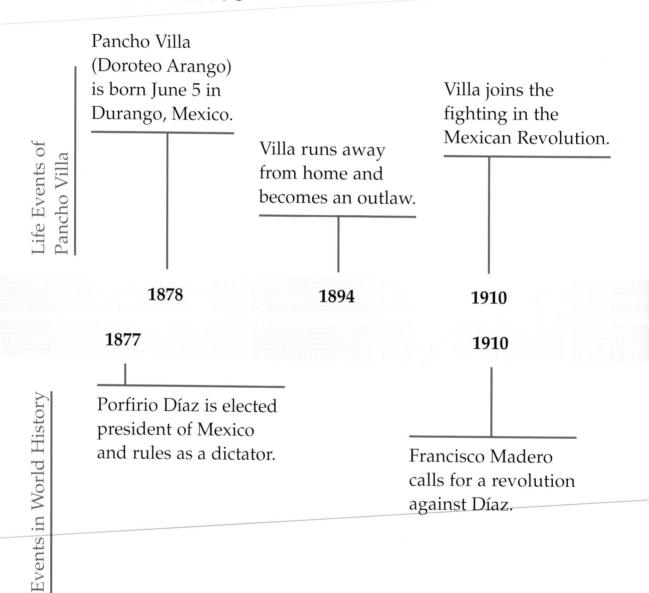

Life Events of Pancho Villa

Pancho Villa (Doroteo Arango) is born June 5 in Durango, Mexico.

1878

Villa runs away from home and becomes an outlaw.

1894

Villa joins the fighting in the Mexican Revolution.

1910

Events in World History

1877

Porfirio Díaz is elected president of Mexico and rules as a dictator.

1910

Francisco Madero calls for a revolution against Díaz.

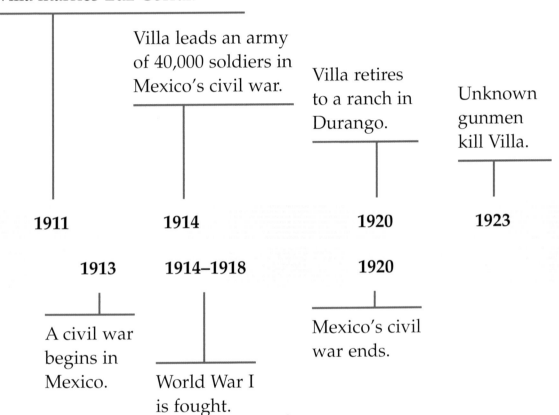

Villa and Pascual Orozco take control of Ciudad Juárez and force President Díaz to resign; Villa marries Luz Corral.

Villa leads an army of 40,000 soldiers in Mexico's civil war.

Villa retires to a ranch in Durango.

Unknown gunmen kill Villa.

1911

1914

1920

1923

1913

1914–1918

1920

A civil war begins in Mexico.

World War I is fought.

Mexico's civil war ends.

Glossary

credit (KRED-it)—a way of buying something without using money; the debt is paid later.

outlaw (OUT-law)—a criminal, especially one who is running away from the law

pension (PEN-shuhn)—an amount of money paid regularly to someone who has retired from work

rebel (REB-uhl)—someone who fights against a government or against the people in charge of something

revolution (rev-uh-LOO-shuhn)—a violent uprising by the people of a country that changes its system of government

telegraph (TEL-uh-graf)—an instrument that uses electrical signals to send messages over wires

Internet Sites

FactHound offers a safe, fun way to find Internet sites related to this book. All of the sites on FactHound have been researched by our staff.

Here's how:

1. Visit *www.facthound.com*
2. Type in this special code **073685441X** for age-appropriate sites. Or enter a search word related to this book for a more general search.
3. Click on the **Fetch It** button.

FactHound will fetch the best sites for you!

Read More

Hodgkins, Fran. *Mexico: A Question and Answer Book.* Fact Finders. Questions and Answers. Countries. Mankato, Minn.: Capstone Press, 2005.

Marcovitz, Hal. *Pancho Villa.* The Great Hispanic Heritage. Philadelphia: Chelsea House, 2003.

Stein, R. Conrad. *Pancho Villa: Mexican Revolutionary Hero.* Proud Heritage. Chanhassen, Minn.: Child's World, 2004.

Index

Arango, Doroteo. *See* Villa, Francisco "Pancho"

Chihuahua, Mexico, 10, 16, 20
Ciudad Juárez, Mexico, 4, 5, 19
civil war, 20
Columbus, New Mexico, 22

Díaz, Porfirio, 6, 16, 18, 19
Durango, 8, 15, 23

farmers, 6, 8, 9, 10, 18

government, 4, 19, 26

Huerta, Victoriano, 20

Madero, Francisco, 16, 17, 18, 19, 20
Mexican Army, 15

Obregón, Álvaro, 23
Orozco, Pascual, 4, 19

rebels, 4, 5, 19, 26
revolution, 7, 18–19, 26

United States, 18, 22, 23

Villa, Francisco "Pancho"
    birth of, 8
    as businessperson, 20
    childhood of, 8, 10
    death of, 24
    education of, 8
    name, 8, 15
    as outlaw, 7, 14–15
    parents of, 8, 10, 12
    as rebel, 4, 18–19, 20, 22–23
    retirement of, 23
    siblings of, 8, 10, 12, 20
    and stories, 12
Villa, Luz Corral (wife), 20, 21

workers, 6, 9, 18, 26